Bird Food Recipes

Rhonda Massingham Hart

CONTENTS

Introduction 2

Natural Menus...3

Bird Feeders..5

Troubleshooting...8

Dietary Demands 10

Personal Preferences 11

Seasonal Feeding...14

Recipes and Food Preparation......................................19

    Suet Mixtures 20

    Bakery Goods...22

    Custom Seed Mixes 23

    A Special Craving 25

    Serves Up! 25

    Special Requests 26

Orphan Birds 29

Feeding Baby 31

Introduction

Just outside your frost-framed windows, half a dozen fat, squabbling chickadees heartily partake of this morning's offering. You smile to yourself. Not only do you enjoy the company of your feathered friends, but you also have the satisfaction of giving Nature a hand when she needs it most.

Feeding wild birds is a wonderful way to enjoy and study nature. Millions of people every year set out winter feeders to entice winged wildlife to their backyards. Some of these feeders are gleefully accepted by hordes of hungry birds, some are patronized, but much of the food is never consumed, and still others are virtually ignored. Is there some secret to luring birds to your feeder?

A basic understanding of a wild bird's needs will make any bird-feeding venture more successful. His first concern is for safety. He will not approach a feeder that in any way appears threatening. Nearby cover, such as dense trees or a pile of brush, should be provided for nervous customers, and the feed must be placed well out of reach of any prowling cats or other predators. Birds are creatures of instinct and habit. Once they have established a routine flight pattern, you must provide a more attactive alternative if you expect them to include your feeder in their schedule. Nesting sites, either natural or man-made, may invite birds to remain in your yard. A supply of natural food sources, such as fruit- or nut-bearing trees or shrubs, will also find favor among the feathered. A reliable supply of water, especially during extreme weather conditions, is highly appreciated.

Though most folks associate bird feeding with the ravages of winter, getting the most from your feeder really means offering prime goodies all year round. This is what makes some feeders the main attraction. Having a regular stop, well-stocked with easy pickin's, may well be the reason many birds choose to overwinter, but it can also keep yearly residents interested throughout the seasons.

The types of birds that come to your feeder will depend on your geographic location, the time of year, and the types of feeders and food you provide. Different birds have different feeding habits, and a variety of food and feeders will attract the most diverse variety of takers.

Natural Menus

Seed Eaters. Most songbirds belong to this broad category. Many eat a combination of seeds and bugs, depending on the time of year. Finches, cardinals, grosbeaks, and sparrows are but a few of the primarily seed-eating birds that are attracted to feeders.

Some Prefer Fruit. Birds that might otherwise ignore your feeders, such as Bohemian and cedar waxwings, orioles, or mockingbirds, can often be bribed with orange halves, apple pieces, or other fruit. Sometimes these offerings take a while to be noticed. Don't give up if the first few offerings are not instantly devoured.

Bugs for Supper. Bug eaters, such as woodpeckers, nuthatches, and robins, may show little interest in your feeders. But come winter they will flock to suet and suet substitutes. Tempt them in the spring with a squirmy tray of mealworms. Most seed eaters will also indulge in insects in the spring when they are raising young.

Some Sip Nectar. Hummingbirds are a delightful addition to any yard. They are primarily attracted to natural food sources, such as flowers and blooming vines and shrubs. They also feed on tiny soft insects found among these blossoms. Hummingbirds will visit nectar feeders on a regular basis if they are kept filled, clean, and free from pests, such as yellow jackets. Also, fruit-loving warblers, orioles, tanagers, and grosbeaks have a taste for the sweet nectar solutions.

Natural Food Sources to Attract Birds

Plant	Birds Attracted
Black cherry	Blue jay, cardinal, downy woodpecker, goldfinch, mockingbird, robin, others
Black walnut	Blue jay, cardinal, downy woodpecker, others
Blueberry	Black-capped chickadee, blue jay, cardinal, robin, mourning dove, starling, scores more
Brambles	Blue jay, cardinal, mockingbird, robin, others
Chokecherry	Black-capped chickadee, blue jay, cardinal, downy woodpecker, goldfinch, mockingbird, robin, others
Dogwood	Cardinal, mockingbird, robin, others
E. White Pine	Black-capped chicadee, blue jay, cardinal, goldfinch, mourning dove, nuthatch, others
Elderberry	Blue jay, cardinal, goldfinch, mockingbird, mourning dove, robin, titmouse, white-breasted nuthatch, others
Gooseberry	Mourning dove, mockingbird, robin, others
Grape	Blue jay, cardinal, goldfinch, mockingbird, robin, mourning dove, others
Hackberry	Cardinal, mockingbird, robin, others
Hawthorn	Blue jay, cardinal, mockingbird, robin, more
Holly	Cardinal, mockingbird, robin, many more
Honeysuckle	Goldfinch, mockingbird, robin, others
Huckleberry	Blue jay, mourning dove, robin, others
Juniper	Downy woodpecker, mockingbird, robin, others
Mountain ash	Robin, white-breasted nuthatch
Maple	Cardinal, goldfinch, robin, others
Mulberry	Blue jay; cardinal; catbird; downy, red-bellied and red-headed woodpeckers; cedar waxwing; eastern kingbird; goldfinch; mockingbird; purple finch; red-eyed vireo; robin; scarlet tanager; wood thrush; yellowbilled cuckoo; many, many others
Multifora rose	Cardinal, mockingbird, others
Oak	Blue jay, cardinal, downy woodpecker, mourning dove, white-breasted nuthatch, others
Olive	Black-capped chickadee, cardinal, mockingbird, mourning dove, robin, others
Red cedar	Cardinal, cedar waxwing, mockingbird, mourning dove, robin, others
Sassafras	Bobwhite, catbird, eastern kingbird, red-eyed vireo, robin
Serviceberry	Blue jay, cardinal, downy woodpecker, goldfinch, mockingbird, mourning dove, robin, others
Sumac	Bobwhite, cardinal, Carolina chickadee, eastern towhee, flicker, goldfinch, mockingbird, phoebe, robin, thrushes, warblers, white-eyed vireo, others
Sunflower	At least 42 species
Sweet gum	Black-capped chickadee, cardinal, goldfinch, others
Virginia creeper	Black-capped chickadee, mockingbird, robin, tufted titmouse, white-breasted nuthatch

Garden flowers, such as bachelor buttons, calendula, California poppy, campanula, chrysanthemum, cone flower, coreopsis, cosmos, dusty miller, marigold, phlox, verbena, and zinnia, among others, also attract an array of birds.

FAVORITE HUMMINGBIRD PLANTS	
Trees	Hawthorn, flowering crabapple, black locust
Bushes	Azalea, butterfly bush, coralberry, flowering currant, flowering quince, hibiscus, red elderberry, weigela
Vines	Clematis, morning glory, scarlet runner bean, trumpet vine, trumpet honeysuckle
Flowers:	
Perennials	Bee balm, bleeding heart, columbine, coral bells, dahlia, day lily, delphinium, foxglove, hollyhock, lupine
Annuals	Dianthus (pinks), flowering tobacco, fuchsia, geranium, impatiens, nasturtium, petunia, salvia

Bird Feeders

Bird feeders come in several types, each designed to serve a specific purpose. Selective feeders discourage nuisance-type birds, such as starlings, crows, and house sparrows. These feeders have very short or no perches, which makes feeding difficult to impossible for chunky visitors, while inviting small, agile birds, such as chickadees, finches, and nuthatches to enjoy a free meal. Non-selective feeders welcome one and all. Any large, accessible feeder with plenty of parking space may be considered a non-selective feeder. While selective feeders are hung from a branch or line to prevent certain birds from feeding, non-selective feeders can cater to ground birds as well as those that prefer to dine higher up.

Other distinctions in feeders include the type of feed they dispense and the manner in which they release it. Hopper feeders funnel seed down into a feeding tray until the hopper bin is empty. They can accommodate different sized seed and usually have clear sides so that you can monitor the contents. They may be set on a stump, tabletop, or windowsill, attached to a post or hung from branches, eaves, or a pulley string. The latter allows you to reel the feeder in for refills or to gradually move it closer to the window for viewing, as the birds become accustomed to its position. These feeders require very little upkeep as they are virtually self-cleaning. If for some reason the level of food does not go down within a few days, check to be sure the seed is not moldy.

Tube feeders are clear plastic cylinders often designed to release seed at several outlets. They are selective feeders that hang freely and sway with the breeze or the weight of perching birds; conditions which discourage larger birds but beckon to small chickadees, house finches, and others. Shortening the perches to H inch will limit accessibility to only the smallest customers. Specialized tube feeders dispense tiny thistle (niger) seed, highly prized by goldfinches and siskins, one seed at a time. This is perfectly suited to their habit of flying to a safe place with each seed they find before eating it.

A tray or platform-type feeder can be set near or at ground level to entice a nearly limitless variety of birds. It can hold anything from seeds and nuts to fruit and suet. It is a non-selective type feeder, allowing for the greatest possible variety of birds.

Suet feeders are specially made to hold solid suet or suet mixtures or substitutes. They can be as simple as a hanging mesh bag (such as an onions or oranges bag), a piece of hardware cloth bent to shape and nailed in place, or a large pine cone smeared with fat. Fancier versions can be store bought or created from small logs with holes bored to hold the suet.

Nectar feeders are almost exclusively for hummingbirds. They are clear plastic and usually have red parts to attract the hummer's attention. These feed a sweet liquid mixture through a narrow tube or several small openings.

Drawing a variety of birds to your yard requires consideration of the type of feed you will offer and how you will offer it. Selective feeders attract small seed eaters. Non-selective tray feeders may attract anything, including crows, starlings, sparrows, and squirrels, which can all make considerable nuisances of themselves. Suet feeders bring in bug eaters and are especially important in the winter when energy requirements are up and available nutrients are scarce.

The height at which a feeder is placed also influences who will make use of it. Many seed-eating birds are strictly ground feeders. Quail, pheasants, and doves feed at ground level and generally prefer cracked corn and white millet. Some birds prefer to eat a few feet off the ground. These are fruit-eating or varied-diet birds, such as waxwings or jays. Some bug eaters, such as nuthatches and titmice, look for food even higher up. Tree trunk feeders, such as woodpeckers, nuthatches, flickers, sapsuckers, kinglets, and creepers, search primarily for insects along the trunks of trees. Hummingbirds feed on the wing from ground level to 10 feet or higher.

FEEDING HEIGHT PREFERENCES

Ground Feeders	Tabletop	Hanging or Post	Tree Trunk
Chickadees	Chickadees	Chickadees	Flickers
Jays	Jays	Titmice	Woodpeckers
Game birds	Waxwings	Nuthatches	Sapsuckers
Robins	Grosbeaks	Grosbeaks	Chickadees
Starlings	Starlings	Finches	Nuthatches
Towhees	Finches	Redpolls	Creepers
Sparrows	Redpolls	Siskins	Kinglets
Juncos	Hummingbirds	Hummingbirds	
Cardinals	Cardinals		
Mourning doves			
Pigeons			
Crows			
Cowbirds			
Grackles			
Red-winged blackbirds			

Feeder Tips

Here are some tips to help make your bird feeders successful:
- Place feeders so they are easily visible, both by you and the birds. Birds won't eat what they can't see.
- Birds prefer to eat in the sun, but out of direct wind and weather.
- Place near cover.
- Avoid placing directly in front of windows; to the side is better. Birds can be warned away from otherwise invisible glass by closing curtains or putting stickers in windows.
- Use a variety of feeders and food.
- Keep feeders clean and full. Fill at the same time each day.

Troubleshooting

Trilling songbirds and brightly feathered visitors are not the only ones to frequent bird feeders. There are a number of other creatures that can make pests of themselves and in some cases even scare away the birds you are trying to encourage.

Squirrels. Public enemy number one to many bird feeders. They steal or waste food and can damage or destroy feeders in their zeal to empty them. Hang pie pans, metal lids, even old phonograph records up and down support wires of hanging feeders. Use short sections of garden hose or tubing as spacers. Use chew-proof wire. Place feeders at least 8 feet from any take-off point hungry squirrels may try to use. Try suspending feeders from a horizontal line that has been strung with tubing, old plastic pop bottles, or other obstacles. Baffles, spinners, cones, and other barriers are commercially available.

Cats. Provide nearby cover, but keep the immediate area clear so that cats can't sneak up on the feeder undetected. Bell your cat or keep it inside, especially during nesting season. Fence around the feeder area with a 2- to 3-foot tall fence of hardware cloth or chicken wire.

Starlings or House Sparrows. Offer selective feeders with short or no perches, and hang them so they swing freely. Try a counter-balance feeder, which is designed so that the weight of a heavy bird causes the food door to close. Arrange suet feeders so that the only access to the suet is for the bird to hang upside down. Avoid foods that attract these birds, such as baked goods, table scraps, and peanut hearts, and opt for sunflower and millet, if these birds become a nuisance. If the problem becomes severe stop ground or platform feeding for awhile.

Rodents. Don't overstock ground feeders, offer only as much as the birds will finish each day. Clean up leftovers and cut down on spilled waste by eliminating commercial seed mixes.

Hawks. Once birds begin to congregate regularly around your feeders, they may attract the attention of such birds of prey as Coopers or sharp-skinned hawks. Help protect your invited guests by providing nearby cover.

See-thru Trolley Birdfeeder

The "food house" makes birds feel right at home, with a roof and four walls. This type of house may have one or more glass panels to provide a closer look. When attached to a rope line with a pulley, you can draw the house a bit closer each day to a really good bird-watching vantage point.

The Corn Feeder

In rural areas, or on the fringes of suburbs, if your favorites are the quail, pheasant, and grouse, even these shy birds will come out of hiding to feast at your corn feeder. This is a type of feeding shelf where the corn is set on spikes driven upward through a board. These shelves should be placed under or near hedges just above snowline. Expect a visit from rabbits and squirrels — they find such low level feeders irresistible.

Seed and Suet Ball

Mold a mixture of seeds and melted suet into a ball. Let it harden. Place the ball in a loosely knitted twine or yarn sack for support. Do not use wire or other metal — in extreme cold the moist tongue or eye of the bird may stick to the frosted metal. Hang the ball from the porch or a tree branch.

Hopper Feeder

The simple hopper feeder is useful because it holds a large supply of feed, and guards it from contamination. The hopper also serves the feed easily and economically.

Window Shield

The window shield is the kind of feeder station most commonly used. This shelf can also be placed on a tree or pole. It is best to put the shelf in a sunny window on a protected side of the house. To prevent the wind from sweeping the tray clean, a raised ledge may be added.

Milk Carton Feeder

Empty milk cartons make good bird feeders.
Source: Oregon Fish & Wildlife

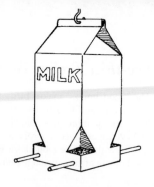

Dietary Demands

The nutritional demands of wild birds vary with the season. Even in sub-freezing weather small birds must maintain a body temperature of 105°F. In any season a bird's dietary requirements are substantial. To "eat like a bird" literally means to fill much of every waking hour in the pursuit of food.

To insure the overall success and effectiveness of your feeding program it is important to have an understanding of the comparative attractiveness and nutritional value of bird foods. Some foods, suet and nuts in particular, are especially high in fat and calories, and are considered "heating foods." Others, like torn white bread or doughnut pieces, seem to be universally favored by many birds, but fall short nutritionally. Even so, they are valuable in establishing a feeder and enticing visiting birds to sample other, healthier offerings.

ATTRACTIVENESS AND NUTRITIONAL VALUE

Food	Attractiveness	Nutrition
White bread	High to most birds	Low to moderate
Cornbread	Moderate	Moderate to good
Doughnuts	Moderate to good	Low
White proso millet	High, especially sparrows and juncos	High
Black-oil sunflower	High; many prefer to white millet	Most nutritious of the sunflower seeds
Red proso millet	High	Similar to white millet
Shelled peanuts	High	Rich in protein and calories
Black-striped sunflower	Moderate	Good
Canary seed	Moderate, eaten by birds that like white proso millet	Moderate in protein and minerals
Hulled sunflower	Moderate	High
Milo	Low; a common "filler" in commercial mixes, often scratched aside	Moderate

Food	Attractiveness	Nutrition
Gray-striped sunflower	Low	Less oil than others
Buckwheat	Low; except to doves	Moderate
Thistle (niger)	Low; except to goldfinches, siskins, and other finches	High
Rice	Low	Poor
Peanut hearts	Low; except to starlings	High, spoils easily
Oat groats	Low	Good
Flax	Nearly worthless	Moderate
Rape	Very few takers	High fat, protein, and minerals
Corn	High	High, vitamin A, protein
Nutmeats	High	Rich in heat and calories
American cheese	Very appealing to some	High
Cottage cheese	High for young birds	High
Apples	High to many types	Moderate
Berries	High	Good
Orange halves	High to some	Good
Suet	High	High
Peanut butter	High	High

Personal Preferences

All wild birds have common requirements that you can offer to attract their attention: water, salt, and grit. These are in short supply during cold weather as water freezes up and sandy patches get snowed over.

A clean bird bath (with an inclined floor) is a welcome stop to both drinkers and bathers. Many birds like to eat their food with water. Salt should be offered mixed with other food as it is often ignored if set out alone. Grit is necessary for birds to grind the food they eat and for some mineral value. Offer ground oyster shell, sand, or ground eggshell either alone in trays or mixed with seed or recipes.

The list of other possible offerings is nearly limitless. Some items have a wide appeal, while others are relished by some and rejected by others. Many birds have definite preferences which you can use to tailor your feeding program to include your favorite species. Some foods attract a wide variety of birds and are helpful in establishing business at a new feeder.

Favorite Foods of Favorite Birds

Bird	Fruit	Seed
Black-capped chickadee and Titmice		canary, corn, hemp, melon, thistle, oats, pumpkin, squash, sunflower
Bluebird	baked apples, currants, figs, grapes, raisins, strawberries	
Blue Jay	apples, raisins	hemp, melon, safflower, sunflower, whole or cracked corn
Cardinal		sunflower, cracked corn, buckwheat
Cedar Waxwing	apples, cherries, currants, grapes, raisins	sunflower
Dark-eyed Junco		canary, pumpkin, hemp, white millet, cracked corn, squash, sunflower, thistle
Evening and other Grosbeaks		apple seeds, cracked corn, melon, millet, safflower, soybean, sunflower
Grouse, Quail, Pheasant		whole or cracked corn, whole oats, soybean
Goldfinch		cracked corn, canary, while proso millet, black sunflower, thistle
Mockingbird	apples, bananas, currants, figs, dates, grapes, oranges, raisins, pears, strawberries, watermelon	
Mourning Dove	peanut hearts, pecans	
Northern Oriole	apples, bananas, oranges, grapes, raisins, watermelon	cracked corn, millet, rice
Nuthatch		cantaloupe, melon, sunflower
Pine siskin		sunflower, thistle
Red-winged Blackbird		buckwheat, canary, millet, niger, oats, whole or cracked corn, sunflower
Robin	blueberries, cherries, currants, apples, grapes, pears, raisins, strawberries	
Rufus-sided Towhee	grapes	barley, canary, cracked corn, hemp, millet, thistle, oats, sunflower
Scarlet Tanager	apples, bananas, cherries, oranges, raisins	
Starling	apples, currants, grapefruit raisins	cracked or canned corn, melon, milo, oat groats, wheel oats, cooked rice
Stellars Jay		corn
Woodpecker		cracked corn, shelled sunflower

Peanut butter should never be served straight as it can stick to a bird's beak.

Protein	**Other**
n drippings, meat scraps, almonds, ernuts, coconut**, hickory, peanuts, ns, walnuts, peanut butter*	white bread, cornmeal, dog biscuit, doughnuts, pie crust
ge cheese	biscuits, doughnuts, pie crust
n drippings, cooked eggs, meat ps, suet, peanuts, peanut butter*, ut hearts, pecans, walnuts	cooked potatoes, potato peelings, white bread, cornbread, cracker crumbs, dog biscuits, doughnuts, chicken feed, eggshells
ut butter*, peanut hearts, suet, ns, black walnut, rolled oats	white bread, cornbread, dog biscuit, doughnut, pie crust, chicken feed
, peanuts, peanut ts, pecans	sugar water
	chicken feed, white bread
, hickory nut, peanut butter*, ut hearts, English walnuts	chicken feed
, cooked eggs, peanut butter*, ut hearts	white bread, cornbread, doughnuts
kwheat, canary, whole or cracked corn, p, melon, white proso millet, le, milo, oat, sunflower	chicken feed
, peanut butter*, pecans	honey, jelly, sugar water, syrup, white bread, doughnut, pie crust
n drippings, suet, almonds, butternut, ut, peanut butter*, peanut heart, k walnut	white bread, doughnut
	salt, ashes
, peanut hearts, pped pecans	chicken feed, white bread, cornbread
, American cheese, peanut er*, peanut hearts, pecans	biscuits, white bread, cornbread, doughnuts, cooked spaghetti
, peanut hearts	chicken feed, white bread, dog biscuit
	sugar water, white bread
n drippings, cooked eggs, meat scraps, , American cheese, peanut butter*, ut hearts, canned dog food	alfalfa meal, white bread, cornbread, dog biscuit, doughnuts, potato chips, boiled potatoes, cooked sweet potatoes, sauerkraut
t scraps, peanut butter*, suet, lish walnuts	white bread
t scraps, suet, almonds, coconut**, ory nuts, peanuts, black walnuts	cornbread, doughnuts

ver offer dried, shredded coconut as it swells once inside the bird.

Seasonal Feeding

Spring

The need for supplemental feeding is at its peak in the early spring. By now the natural foods available from the previous season are long gone, and the current season's growth has not yet started. Birds are about to nest and lay eggs, putting further strain on their winter-weakened bodies. Egg laying requires a high level of calcium which can be supplied with crushed eggshells or ground oyster shell.

Summer

Even though natural foods are plentiful in the summer, there is still much you can do to entice birds to come to your feeder. During this season birds must feed not only themselves but their rapidly growing young. This rapid growth demands lots of protein, which turns even the most placid seed eaters into determined bug hunters.

There are several ways you can meet the nutritional demands of summer. Cut down on high energy, heat-producing foods such as suet and nutmeats. Or go a little buggy! Mealworms, the larvae of the Tenebrio molitor beetle, are commercially available, easily homegrown, and irresistible to many kinds of birds.

Fledgling Foods. If you feed birds year 'round, those that raise their young in your vicinity may bring their babies to your feeders. This requires an extreme amount of trust on the part of the birds, for if they have even one frightening experience at your feeder they may never return, let alone bring their fledglings. So sell or bell the cat, keep the field of vision clear, have some cover nearby, and put out some special goodies for the kids.

Nestlings are raised on a partially pre-digested "bug stew." New foods should be soft textured and mild tasting. Offer some of the following dishes to introduce fledglings to new foods while establishing their trust in you and your feeders. Since suet may turn rancid, use the summer suet substitute in very warm weather.

COTTAGE CHEESE SALAD

**Currants, raisins, blueberries,   Cottage cheese
grapes, or mulberries**

Stir fruit into cottage cheese and set out in shallow containers. Don't set out more than the birds will eat in a day. Better to refill several times a day than to let the salad spoil.

BABY BREAD

Sugar   Milk   White bread

Stir a little sugar into milk until dissolved. Cut bread into pieces and soak in the sweetened milk for a few seconds. Set pieces on feeding tray.

CORNMEAL MUSH

1 part water

Salt

Choice of fruit: **Mashed bananas, strawberries, cherries, blueberries, or preserves**

4 parts water

1 part cornmeal

For leftovers:

Flour

Shortening or bacon drippings

Mix 1 part water with cornmeal. Bring 4 parts water to a boil and stir in cornmeal mixture and salt. Boil one minute. Remove from heat and pour into serving container, such as an old foil pie plate. Stir in fruit. Chill leftovers, form into patties, dust with flour and fry in shortening or bacon drippings as a treat for older birds.

COOKED CEREAL

**Hot cereal of your choice (oatmeal, wheathearts, Farina, etc.)
Pieces of fruit, berries, preserves, or peanut butter**

Prepare according to cereal directions and stir in additives. Serve as for Cornmeal Mush.

SOFT SUET

The softer texture and extra sweetness is much easier for young birds to swallow.

2 parts suet   ½ part apple or grape jelly   1 part peanut butter

Melt suet and allow to cool until it begins to thicken. Stir in peanut butter and jelly. Pour into containers and set out on feeder tray. Consider nailing them down to avoid grand theft.

SUMMER SUET SUBSTITUTE

1 part flour	Dash salt
1 part peanut butter	1 part vegetable shortening
3 to 4 parts yellow cornmeal	

Mix dry ingredients and stir into gooey. Spoon into containers. Favored by tanagers, thrushes, warblers and many others.

SQUIGGLY WIGGLY STEW

Mealworm larvae*   Various sprouts: Bean, alfalfa, etc.**

Mix in any ratio and set out on feeder tray. The feathers are sure to fly for this highly nutritious combination.

*Raising mealworms is neither expensive nor complicated. It does require quite a devotion to the birds! The "worms" can be grown in any container from a jar, shoebox, or old casserole to an abandoned aquarium. Stock the container with bran and bread crumbs (or cornmeal, Farina, cracker crumbs, etc.) about half full. Place a few slices of apple or potato on top to provide moisture, add bugs, and cover the works with a few layers of old newspaper. Cover the container with a snug-fitting lid, something that will let air in but no bugs out, such as an old pillowcase, crop cover fabric, window screening, or what have you, and secure. Remove the wigglers as needed and replenish the crumb and apple supply every few months.

**Many kinds of seeds can be sprouted for bird feeding and the process of coming to life makes them all the more nutritious. Place seeds, such as mung bean, alfalfa, radish, or other into a jar and soak in warm water overnight. Place a cheese cloth or other well ventilated cover over the jar and drain off the water. Replace with just as much water as it takes to keep the seeds moist. Rinse the seeds and replace the water twice daily until the seeds sprout (2 to 6 days).

Some of the birds of summer are especially fond of fruit — the riper the better. Tanagers, orioles, even some woodpeckers will gladly swoop down to indulge in a sweet fruit salad.

SUMMER FRUIT SALAD

Oranges, halved or quartered
Banana, cut into chunks
Apple, cut into pieces
Black cherries, whole
Seasonal berries, whole
Other fruit as is available

Set out smaller pieces on feeding tray. Impale orange halves and other large pieces on nails driven up through the tray floor.

SUMMER FRUIT TREE

Drive nails into a wooden post and skewer fruit to it, using the same type of ingredients as above.

Summer is also time for hummingbirds. There are some basic rules to consider for their well-being:

- Choose feeders with multiple openings rather than a single tube.

- Some parts of the feeder should be red to attract attention.

- Keep feeders clean. Bacterial and fungal growth can be debilitating to the birds. Rinse thoroughly every few days with hot tap water and scrub with a bottle brush, hot water and a little white vinegar, not soap or detergent.

Although honey is more nutritious than plain sugar water it is also much more susceptible to spoilage and contains botulism toxins. Molds form quickly, which can infect the hum-mingbird's tongues. The birds cannot feed and soon perish. Therefore, honey/water solutions are not recommended.

Too strong of a sugar solution can be harmful. Concentrations of more than 1 part sugar to 4 parts water can cause liver enlargement and subsequent liver failure.

To prepare homemade hummingbird nectar either white or brown sugar can be used. Never use artificial sweeteners, as they contain no calories and will quickly starve the birds to death.

Once the hummers become regular customers you may reduce the mix to 1 part sugar to 6 parts water. This further decreases the chance of liver damage and encourages the birds to continue to seek out natural foods. Commercial preparations which contain vitamins and minerals are also available.

HUMMINGBIRD NECTAR
Sugar   Water

Mix equal portions of sugar and water and bring to boil. This helps the sugar dissolve completely and retards fermentation. Dilute to a ratio of four to one by adding 1½ parts of cold water per part of sugar mix. Store unused portions in the refrigerator.

Bees or wasps can become troublesome at hummingbird feeders. They can be discouraged by smearing a little petroleum jelly or salad oil around the dispenser holes.

Fall

During autumn young birds are learning to fend for themselves, and migratory birds are preparing for their long flights by putting on as much fat as possible and by molting into a new set of feathers. These transitions are taxing on the birds and demand optimum nutrition if they are to survive the winter. Starting a winter feeding program early in the fall has the added advantage of luring birds to your feeder that might move on further south if you wait until later in the season to start feeding.

Winter

Freezing temperatures, chill winds, snow cover, and lack of natural food make winter the most obvious time to keep bird feeders full. Nights are long and temperatures plummet. A study of chickadees found that they could put on as much as 7.5 percent of their body weight during the day, only to have burned it off by the following morning. Birds will be most active in their search for food first thing in the morning and again just before nightfall. Make sure feeders, water, and grit are accessible at these high-demand times.

Freezing weather places a tremendous energy demand on a wild bird's system. Because of this, high fat/high protein/high energy foods are more important in the winter than any other time of year. They are referred to as "heating foods." Nuts are one example, and suet, the hard, white beef fat found behind the kidneys is a favorite winter offering. It is gratefully accepted by at least eighty different species of North American birds.

Recipes and Food Preparation

Preparing Suet

The simplest way to offer suet is in large raw chunks, suspended in mesh bags or held in wire holders. Suet can also be prepared by melting and cooling. While there is no difference in nutritional value, prepared suet lasts longer, is less likely to spoil during warm temperature lulls, is less appealing to starlings and other pest type birds, and is easy to work with.

- Cut large chunks of suet into smaller pieces or run through meat grinder.
- Melt the pieces over low heat until liquid. Allow to cool in pan until solidified.
- Slowly reheat suet until liquid a second time. At this stage the suet is ready to be poured into molds. It can be poured over or mixed with a variety of other ingredients, or allowed to cool somewhat and spread into drilled log feeders, pine cones, onto tree branches, etc.

Whether served straight or mixed in a recipe, prepared suet lends itself well to a variety of serving forms. Finding suet containers needn't strain your budget, just your imagination. Here are some suggestions:

Muffin tins	Tuna fish or cat food cans
Yogurt cups	Cottage cheese containers
Coconut halves	Log drilled with 1-inch holes
Cake molds formed by	Foil lined cookie pan. Use
folding foil around bars	cookie cutter on hardened
of soap or other forms.	suet to make shapes.

Pine cones can be spread with suet or suet mixtures and hung from tree branches.

Create suet balls by pouring suet into a rounded mold and removing while still warm and soft enough to manipulate. Set on wax paper and press into shape using the wax paper. When cooled, hang in a mesh bag.

Suet Mixtures

All by itself suet is a valuable source of energy and very attractive to many birds. Suet cakes, cones, molds, and mixtures simply liven up the menu and keep the birds interested.

YUMMY CRUMB CAKES

This recipe combines the high energy of suet, the mass appeal of popular seeds and the extra treat of fruit.

1½ parts wheat or multi-grain bread crumbs

1 part hulled sunflower seeds

1 part white or red proso millet

½ part chopped dried fruit (apples, blueberries, raisins, cherries)

6 to 9 parts suet

Dash of salt

Sprinkle of sand

Melt suet, allow to cool, then re-melt. As it cools the second time stir in all other ingredients. Spoon into molds. Once the cakes solidify, place in suet feeders or attach to trays.

HANGING HEAVEN

A rich, nutritious mix, appreciated by a variety of birds, especially in winter. Even the feeder is edible!

3 parts suet

1 part cornmeal

1 part peanut butter

Sprinkling of sand

1 part brown sugar

1 part raisins, dried cherries, etc.

1 or more coconuts, split in half

1 part mixed seed or broken nuts

Melt suet, allow to cool, then re-melt. Stir in other ingredients. Cook until the mixture is the consistency of porridge. If too thick, add small amounts of water or milk; if too thin, add flour. Pour into coconut halves. Hang coconut halves from tree limbs or eaves.

NO SUET SUET

So tasty you might be tempted to try it yourself!

2 cups water

1 tablespoon butter

1 tablespoon sugar

2 tablespoons cinnamon

1 cup oatmeal

½ cup raisins

4 cups crunchy peanut butter

½ cup cornmeal

½ cup whole wheat flour

½ cup millet

Boil water with butter, sugar, and cinnamon. Add oatmeal and raisins. Cook one minute and stir in remaining ingredients. Press into containers or mold directly onto tree branches.

VON BERLEPSH FORMULA

This highly nutritious formula was developed by the National Audubon Society to resemble the natural diet of insect-eating birds. It is very high in protein and energy and heartily consumed by many overwintering species of birds.

5 parts fine, dry bread crumbs	3 parts dried, ground meat
1½ parts dried berries or fruit	5 parts hempseed
3 parts millet or 5 parts ground, dried meat	2 parts ant "eggs"*
	3 parts hulled sunflower seed

Suet

Combine all ingredients except suet. Melt down 1½ times as much suet as the total volume of all other ingredients. This will be equivalent to about 30 parts suet. Allow to cool, then mix with all other ingredients. Allow to cool until of a spreadable consistency. Originally intended to be spread directly onto tree trunks for insect foraging birds, this mixture can also be spread into containers, pie cones, etc. Since the suet is only once melted it will be softer than twice-melted recipes.

*The pupal stage of ants that can be discovered by disturbing ants underneath woodpiles, stumps, etc. If you'd rather forego the foraging part of this recipe, substitute 5 parts ground, dried meat.

FAT & SASSY

This mixture appeals to a variety of birds. It is high in energy and nutrition.

2 parts suet, lard, bacon drippings, or saved kitchen fat

1 part peanut butter

1 to 2 parts yellow cornmeal

1 part fine cracked corn — or millet — or hulled sunflower

Dash of salt and sand

Melt suet over low heat. Allow to cool and harden, then heat again. Stir in peanut butter and other ingredients, reserving some of the corn or seeds. Allow to cool somewhat and pour into molds or form into balls. Roll balls into loose corn or seed.

SWEET SUET CAKES

A sweet treat for your favorite bug eaters.

1 part suet	½ part white flour
6 parts water	1 part brown sugar
2 parts cornmeal	Dash of salt and sand

Bring suet and water to boil. Add cornmeal, flour, sugar, salt and sand. Allow mixture to cool, then pour into molds and allow to harden. Serve on feeder tray or tie to branches.

Bakery Goods

Just like us, many birds have a craving for the sweetness and texture of baked goods. Gratify their "sweet beaks" with some down home baking, just for them.

BETTER BIRDIE BREAD

White bread seems to be a universal favorite of wild birds. Unfortunately, it isn't terribly high in nutrients. Try this rich white bread recipe instead of plain store bought bread.

2	packages yeast	⅓	cup corn oil
½	cup warm water	3	eggs
1½	cups water	2	teaspoons salt
¼	cup honey		7+ cups flour

Dissolve yeast in ½ cup warm water. Set aside. Mix water, honey, oil, eggs, and salt in large bowl. Add dissolved yeast. Stir in flour, first with wooden spoon then using hands. Knead on floured surface 5 minutes. Place in greased bowl and turn so that dough is greased all around. Let rise 1 hour or until dough has doubled in bulk. Punch down and divide into 2 or 3 loaves. Place in greased pans or set on cookie sheets and allow to rise for one more hour. Bake at 375°F for 40 minutes. Crumble to serve.

CORNBREAD

3 cups yellow cornmeal	½ teaspoons baking powder
½ cup seeds, raisins, nuts, dried	⅓ cup shortening or bacon fat
berries, peanut butter, fruit,	3 cups water
or ground meat, optional	Sprinkling of fine sand

Combine all ingredients, adding the seeds, raisins, nuts, dried berries, peanut butter, fruit, or ground meat to add extra zing. Bake at 425°F for 25 minutes, in a well-greased pan. Allow to cool, turn out of pan. Crumble to serve.

FRUIT BREAD

Birds that love fruit, sweets, and bread, such as tanagers and orioles, find this sweet, fruity bread just to their taste.

2 packages yeast (2 tablespoons)	½ cup sugar
¼ cup warm water	2 tablespoons shortening
2½ cups fruit juice (orange,	1 tablespoon salt
apple, raspberry, etc.)	7+ cups flour

Dissolve yeast in warm water. Let sit while combining other ingredients, except flour. Stir yeast into juice mixture. Add flour, mixing first by spoon, then by hand. Turn out on floured surface and let rest about 10 minutes.

Knead about 8 minutes, until surface is smooth and elastic. Divide into loaves and place in greased bread pans. Let rise until doubled in bulk. Bake at 425°F for 25 to 30 minutes. Cool on rack and serve in torn pieces.

NUTTIER FRUITCAKE

2 pounds mixed berries and chopped fruit (white raisins, candied cherries, wild berries, dried cherries, dates, prunes, etc.)	2 cups white flour 1 cup sugar ½ cup shortening 1 teaspoon baking powder ½ teaspoon vanilla
1 pound mixed chopped nuts (pecans, walnuts, peanuts, wild nuts)	4 egg whites ½ cup milk 1 teaspoon fine sand

Dredge fruit and nuts with ½ cup flour. Set aside. Cream sugar and shortening. Alternately add milk and flour mixed with baking powder, stirring between each addition. Stir in vanilla, fruit, nuts, and sand. Beat egg whites stiff and fold in. Spoon into greased baking dish (a round tube pan 10 x 4½ inches is best) and bake 1 hour at 300°F. Crumble to serve.

SCRAP PIE

A great way to use up a lot of leftovers. A variety of birds welcome this hearty, wholesome entree.

4 cups crumbs (bread, cookie, cake, doughnut, etc.)	¼ cup honey ½ teaspoon salt
4 cups kitchen scraps (noodles, meat scraps, fruit, or vegetables, etc.), chopped	1 teaspoon fine sand 2 cups milk 2 tablespoons shortening or melted bacon fat
4 eggs	

Grease baking pan and layer bread crumbs and scraps. Beat eggs and mix with remaining ingredients. Pour over crumbs and scraps. Cover and chill for 1 to 3 hours, then bake at 325°F for 1 hour. Cool and crumble to serve.

Custom Seed Mixes

Most commercial mixes contain a large amount of "filler" seed, such as milo or wheat. While not totally lacking in nutrition, these seeds are not of much value because many birds scratch them aside. Good commercial mixes contain sunflower, safflower, white or red proso millet, cracked corn and even peanuts. If you can't find a mix to suit your particular clientele, whip up a batch of your own.

50/50

A simple combination sure to draw a crowd.

Black oil-type sunflower seed

Cracked corn

Combine equal parts of each and set out at ground level or in elevated feeders.

GAME BIRD FAME

You will be famous with a variety of game birds and other ground feeders in your areas if you serve this irresistible mixture of their favorites.

2 parts chicken scratch	**2 parts whole corn**
1 part whole oats	**1 part buckwheat**
1 part soybean seeds	**1 teaspoon grit per quart of seed**

Combine ingredients and offer at ground level. Be sure there is nearby cover to allow shy birds a chance to retreat if they feel threatened.

COME ONE, COME ALL

A healthy mix with vast appeal.

3 parts sunflower seed	**3 parts hempseed**
3 parts millet	**1 part canary seed**
1 part finely cracked corn	**Grit**

Mix and offer at any level.

GRANOLA CRUNCH

The variety in this recipe makes it appealing to many kinds of birds. Use the main ingredients, but don't hesitate to substitute or toss in leftovers, such as bread or cake crumbs, pie crust pieces, dried fruit, cracked corn, or what-have-you. Combine the finished granola with suet for a woodpecker treat.

1 part honey	**1 part wheat germ**
1 part corn or peanut oil	**2 parts raisins or dried berries**
2 parts chopped peanuts	**2 parts hulled sunflower seed**
2 parts white proso millet	**2 parts crumbled dog biscuits**

Mix and heat honey and oil. In large bowl combine all other ingredients and pour heated liquid over them. Mix and press into shallow pan. Bake at 375°F for 10 minutes. Crumble to serve.

A Special Craving

Many birds regularly risk their lives to glean salt and minerals from roadways. Here is a safer alternative that rewards you for your thoughtfulness with flocks of lingering birds.

CRYSTALLINE

Salt
Wood ashes*

Mix salt and ashes with enough water to dissolve and pour over a large rock, stump or wood block. As the water evaporates, crystals form that attract mineral-hungry birds.

*These can be fireplace ashes as long as they do not contain residues from burning colored (especially red) or slick finished paper.

Serves Up!

Sometimes the simplest fare can be made intriguing by the way in which it is served. Try these fun favorites.

Corn on the Cob on a Spike. First prepare the dining table. Drive several large nails through an old plank or mill end. Old, weathered wood blends into the surroundings better, both in scent and sight, and is less startling to shy ground-feeding birds. Grease each spike with shortening or salad oil and push an ear of corn (fresh or dried) over each. Set out at ground level near cover.

String 'em Along. Especially appropriate at Christmastime are decorative strands of whole peanuts, popcorn, caramel corn, dried or fresh berries, pieces of fruit, etc. Wrap around trees, hang from window to feeder, weave into holiday wreaths and watch the birds cheerfully dismantle them.

Gourmet Bouquet. Of the many trees, shrubs, and plants that appeal to birds, chances are that you have only a few in your yard. Don't despair. Ask friends and neighbors for cuttings or trimmings of the birds' beloved branches. (See table on page 4) Collect them when in fruit or seed and arrange them in a bowl or vase on or near the feeding tray. Push the stems into florist styrofoam or a melon to secure.

Special Requests

Here are some recipes to cater to unique individual cravings.

ROBIN ROUNDS
Perhaps cooked spaghetti reminds the robin of early worms.

Cooked spaghetti   Sprinkling of sand

American cheese, cut in strips   Suet

Chopped apple

Arrange loops of spaghetti in papered muffin tins. Add cheese and apple and sprinkle with sand. Pour melted suet over mixture and allow to cool. Set out at ground level.

BLUE JAY EGGS
Blue jays love eggs, but they may have to share this specialty of the house with mockingbirds, catbirds, or others.

Bacon drippings   Peanut kernels

Eggs   Dash of salt

Apple pieces   Raisins, pecans (optional)

Melt bacon drippings and break in eggs, crumbling in shells. Scramble with apple, peanuts, and salt. Add raisins, pecans, or other favorite jay tidbits. Offer at ground feeder.

DOVE LOVE
Unlike most ground feeders, doves delight in thistle seed. This seed mix will also attract attention from many other birds.

Pecan pieces   Thistle seed

White proso millet   Buckwheat

Cracked corn

Mix in any proportions and scatter on ground.

GOLDFINCH GLORY
Suet   Millet   Thistle seed   Hempseed

Pour twice-melted suet over a mixture of these favorite seeds and cool. Place at feeder.

CARDINAL CANDY

½ part green grapes   1 part sunflower seeds

½ part blueberries   1 part cracked corn

or black cherries   Suet

1 part breadcrumbs   Sprinkle of sand

Arrange all ingredients except suet and sand at bottom of foil pan. Melt, cool, and re-melt suet. Pour over other ingredients. As mixture cools, sprinkle with sand and mix well. Place on ground feeder when cool.

BLUEBIRD HAPPINESS

Bluebirds prefer their apples baked.

1½ cups flour	½ cup shortening
½ teaspoon salt	1 apple, sliced and chopped
Sprinkling of fine sand	½ cup raisins
½ cup sugar	¼ cup water

Combine flour, salt, and sand. Set aside. Bring sugar, shortening, apple, and raisins to boil in water and cook 5 minutes. Combine with flour mixture. Bake at 350°F for 20 minutes. Cook, crumble, and serve at elevated feeder.

CHICKADEELIGHT

Also readily taken by titmice and a number of other birds.

1 part suet	1 part nut pieces (almonds,
Bacon drippings	peanuts, pecans, walnuts)
Chopped meat	1 part sunflower seeds

Melt suet and stir in bacon drippings and meat scraps. Stir in nuts and seeds as mixture cools and thickens. Pour into molds.

Variation: Reserve nuts and seeds. As mixture thickens and cools, fill pine cones. When cones are cooled, spread a second layer of warm suet over them and roll the cones in a mixture of nuts and seeds. Wrap with wax paper and push seeds into suet. Hang from tree branch, feeder, or eaves.

GROSBEAK GOODY

½ cup sunflower seeds	¼ cup cracked corn
¼ cup pecan bits	1 cup suet
¼ cup soybeans	

Stir seeds and nuts into twice-melted suet. Pour into molds or foil-covered cookie sheet. Cut out pieces from hardened mixture on cookie sheet. Place or hang at feeders.

JUNCO JOY

Cracked corn	White bread
Cornmeal	Sprinkling of sand
Canary seed	Peanut butter

Mix dry ingredients and add enough peanut butter to make a spreadable consistency. Spread on white bread. Cut into pieces and serve at feeding tray.

MOCKINGBIRD MUFFINS

2 cups cornmeal	1 cup buttermilk
½ teaspoon soda	1 cup diced meat and fat scraps
¼ teaspoon salt	Sprinkling of sand

Mix all ingredients and pour into greased muffin cups. Bake at 425°F for 20 minutes. Serve at ground or platform feeder.

SISKIN SATISFACTION

| 2 parts hulled sunflower | 1 part salt or wood ashes |
| 2 parts thistle seed | |

Combine ingredients and offer in hanging feeder or elevated tray.

TANAGER TEMPTATION

| Apple or banana pieces | White bread |
| Raisins or cherries | Sugar |

Toss fruit and torn bread with white sugar and offer at ground feeder.

WOODPECKER WONDER
Woodpeckers and flickers will flock to this concoction.

4 parts suet	1 part nut pieces (almonds,
Corn oil	hickory, black walnut, or peanut)
½ part raisins	1 part sunflower seeds
Sprinkling of sand	

Twice melt suet and stir in 1 tablespoon corn oil per cup of suet. Add raisins, seeds, and nuts. When mixture cools to a spreadable consistency spread on tree bark 6 to 10 feet high.

Orphan Birds

A tiny, shivering, featherless lump gawks up at you with unfocused eyes and says, "Yweek!" Now what do you do? The first step in taking care of an orphaned baby bird is to determine whether or not the bird can be returned to its nest. If not, the next step is to ask yourself two very important questions: 1) Are you prepared to cater to this bottomless beak for the next few weeks just as its parents would have? And 2) Can you deal with failure and death or success and release of the foundling into the wild? If you have any hesitation, don't pick that baby up!

Of course you picked it up. Its survival now depends entirely on you, and if you're like most people who don't nurse wild birds to maturity on an everyday basis, you need help. Here are some pointers to help keep you both going:

- Keep baby warm. 92–94°F until pin feathers develop, down to 88°F until fully feathered. Give the baby some control over the temperature by placing it in a towel-lined box with a heat lamp at one end. This way he can move closer to or farther from the heat source. Avoid drafts.
- Weigh baby daily to be sure he gains weight.
- Keep both ends clean. A warm, moist washcloth will do.
- Never attempt to give straight water — babies can drown. They get all the moisture they need from runny formula.

Feeding

Just as finding containers and molds for outdoor feeding takes some recycling imagination, so can finding just the right "bottle" for baby's formula. Depending on the size of the baby a variety of items have been known to serve.

Tiny baby — flat end of toothpick, 1 cc syringe, eyedropper
Medium baby — rubber-coated baby spoon, 3 cc syringe
Big baby — washed-out squeeze mustard bottle, 20 cc (or larger) syringe

Baby formulas must be lump free, warm, and runny. Heat gently over hot water and test the temperature as you would for a human infant. Clean all utensils thoroughly after food preparation and feeding. Birds are very vulnerable to bacteria that develops all too quickily in warm food. Refrigerate leftovers for no more than 2 days. It's better to whip up a fresh batch each morning.

HATCHLING FORMULA

¼ cup water   2 teaspoons Cream of Wheat
Pinch of ground millet*   Hard boiled egg, finely grated

Cook and stir for about 30 seconds; mixture should be runny. Add ground millet and a sprinkling of finely grated hard boiled egg.

*Hulled millet is available in health food stores. Grind in blender and store in air-tight container.

For larger babies progress to more substantial and varied formulas.

BABY FORMULA I

½ cup boiling water   1 teaspoon honey
1 tablespoon wheathearts   1 heaping teaspoon
1 egg yolk   powdered milk
¼ teaspoon ground cuttle-   ½ baby food jar oatmeal with
   bone or oystershell   applesauce and banana

Cook wheathearts in boiling water for 3 to 5 minutes. Add remaining ingredients.

BABY FORMULA II

2½ cups boiling water   1 tablespoon honey
2   teaspoons corn oil   1 baby food jar oatmeal with
½   cup wheathearts   applesauce and bananas
Dash of salt   ⅓ cup sunflower meal
½   cup powdered milk   ¼ teaspoon fine grit

Cook wheathearts with dash of salt in boiling water and corn oil for 3 to 5 minutes. Add remaining ingredients.

BABY FORMULA III

6 cups boiling water   1 cup quick cooking oatmeal
½ cup wheathearts   ½ baby food jar strained peas
½ teaspoon salt   ½ baby food jar strained spinach
1 tablespoon corn oil   ½ baby food jar strained carrots
1 cup powdered milk   ¼ tablespoon fine grit
2 cups sunflower meal

Combine wheathearts, salt, oatmeal, and corn oil in water and cook for 3 to 5 minutes. Add remaining ingredients.

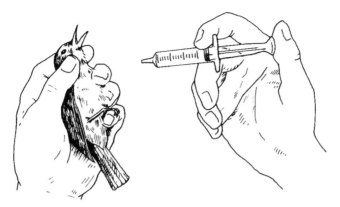

Feeding Baby

In this case a bird in the hand requires gentle care and patience. They really do get the hang of it! The only drawback to this hand feeding is that you get a bird so tame you may want to make a pet of it. Remember, he belongs in the wild.

Follow these steps and you should have baby eating out of your hand and happily gaining weight.

- Feed in a secure place; a table with a soft towel underneath. Hold baby securely, supporting his head.
- Position syringe at the rear of the mouth, just as the mother bird would her beak.
- Gently push a little food into the baby's throat. If he swallows continue until the crop is noticeably expanded. For a tiny finch this may take only a teaspoon of food, for a young crow a half cup. If he doesn't swallow, try again.
- Clean up baby after every meal.
- Check every 2 hours (not at night) and feed when the crop is empty. Failure to empty the crop means a sick bird.
- Better to feed smaller amounts more frequently than too much at once.
- Gradually increase meal amounts while cutting feedings down to 3 to 4 times daily.
- Begin offering soft foods and eventually solids appropriate to the bird's natural diet. Cut down on hand feeding until weaned.

Other Storey Books You Will Enjoy

The Backyard Bird-Lover's Guide by Jan Mahnken
This gorgeously illustrated volume is brimming with information about attracting, enjoying, and understanding 135 of North America's most common species. You'll learn how to feed them, house them, provide nesting materials, and keep them coming back year after year. 320 pages. Paper. ISBN 978-0-88266-927-4.

The Bird Watching Answer Book by Laura Erickson
This portable and convenient reference makes for a knowledgeable companion for any bird enthusiast. With hundreds of questions answered by the experts at the Cornell Lab of Ornithology, you can find information on bird watching techniques and bird behavior like songs, flying, migrating, and much more. 400 pages. Flexibind with paper spine. ISBN 978-1-60342-452-3.

Birdfeeders, Shelters & Baths by Edward A. Baldwin
Learn to control squirrels and other predators while attracting your favorite backyard birds, with more than 25 creative designs for bird-feeders, birdbaths, and more. With step-by-step illustrations, each project is unique and easy to build. 128 pages. Paper. ISBN 978-0-88266-623-5.

Into the Nest by Laura Erickson & Marie Read
Get an intimate look into the family lives of your favorite birds — with beautiful, close-up photography of over 50 birds and their fledglings, nest building, brooding, courtship, and much more. 208 pages. Paper. ISBN 978-1-61212-229-8.

Keeping a Nature Journal
by Clare Walker Leslie & Charles E. Roth
Reconnect with nature with help and guidance from Clare Walker Leslie and Charles Roth. Celebrate the living beauty of each season with these instructional methods to hone your observation skills and help make your journal a work of art. 224 pages. Paper with flaps. ISBN 978-1-58017-493-0.

What's That Bird?
by Joseph Choiniere & Claire Mowbry Golding
With this introductory guide, readers of all ages can learn how to identify common birds and see how birds eat, communicate, and even breathe, as well as learn techniques for observing, journaling, and protecting birds. Your whole family can also enjoy projects such as building a nesting platform, an arbor, and a nesting box. 128 pages. Paper. ISBN 978-1-58017-554-8.

These and other books from Storey Publishing are available wherever quality books are sold or by calling 1-800-441-5700. Visit us at *www.storey.com* or sign up for our newsletter at *www.storey.com/signup*.